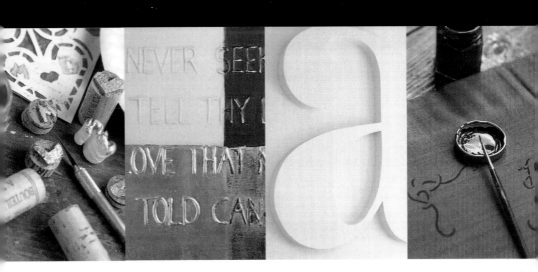

IN YOUR OWN WRITE

IN YOUR

Original photography by
Marie-Louise Avery and Sue Baker

OWN WRITE

Text by JANE FORSTER

A Bulfinch Press Book
Little, Brown and Company
Boston New York Toronto London

AROUND THE HOUSE is intended as a series that will expand into a whole shelf of stylish, practical and focussed handbooks for home decorators. Small enough to be affordable, but long enough to deal with their subjects in depth, they will offer a generous choice of hands-on projects, clearly explained and amplified by excellent, specially-commissioned photographs. If cooks can buy small, subject-specific books such as Pasta, Soups and Salads, why shouldn't decorators be offered the same approach, and choice?

I believe this series – something of a publishing 'first' – will encourage a radical re-think of decorating books, their treatment, format and presentation.

Watch this space!

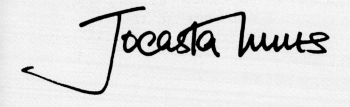

CONTENTS

6 Introduction
8 A Brief History of Lettering
19 Traditional Uses
25 Tools and Materials
28 Useful Hints

31 THE PROJECTS
32 Victorian Valentine
36 Monogrammed Cushions
38 Découpage Bathroom
Frieze
43 Kitchen Labels
46 Victorian Pincushion
48 'Chinese' Lampshade
52 Lettered Lampshade
55 Writing on the Wall
58 Country-style Table Mats
61 Batik Cushions: Homage
to the East
64 Regency-style Muslin
Curtain

68 Decorative Footstool
72 Norwegian Cushion
75 Cupboards: Classic and
Vernacular
78 Silver Gilded Mirror
82 Signwriting:
A Traditional Art
84 Specialist Equipment
for Signwriting

86 Ideas for the Future

87 Gilding Recipes
88 Calligraphy
89 Samples of Lettering Styles

94 Resources and Further
Reading
95 Paint Magic Shops
96 Acknowledgements and
Picture Credits

INTRODUCTION

*I*n this age of the computer, surrounded by the products of an industrial society, we have an increasing appreciation of the handcrafted, and in a world of word processors a passage of beautiful handwriting has a special value. Since its earliest beginnings the written word has always been more than just a way of communicating information. The style of the script adds another depth of meaning to the words, imparting a sense of awe, reverence or delight. Whether we are looking at the classic beauty of Roman inscriptions, the exquisite work of mediaeval manuscripts or the Renaissance elegance of the Humanist minuscule, the work of an individual artist is speaking directly to us. Nowhere is the individual more powerfully felt than through their handwriting. Maybe that is why we find old deeds and letters so fascinating. We can sense the history in John Hancock's signature on the American Declaration of Independence, written in extra-large bold script so that, 'King George III would have no trouble reading it,' and the presence of Elizabeth I in her powerful hand.

Designers are discovering the richness of lettering as a source of inspiration and are using the texture of the writing on old documents, traditional forms of calligraphy and even graffiti to create the style of today. Lettering is treated as pure shape and pattern, allowing new forms and styles to emerge as the evolution of type continues. This book is a response to the growing interests in all the lettering crafts: people are being inspired by the work of artists and designers past and present to explore this creative source for themselves. Once you start looking you will find inspiration for creative lettering all around, and you will start to develop your own personal style. Whether your taste is for the classic scripts of the past or a free modern approach to lettering, here is both inspiration and practical help as you discover the pleasure of designing with letterforms.

The signature of Elizabeth I has all the confidence of a powerful Renaissance monarch. The elaborate flourishes that embellish it leave us in no doubt that this highly educated and cultured woman knew herself to be 'Gloriana'.

A BRIEF HISTORY OF LETTERING

In almost every aspect of modern life we are surrounded by letters, ranging from the precise, formal and legible forms used in the text we read and type to exotic ones that shout at us from advertisements, shop signs and hoardings. In the late twentieth century it is difficult to realize that the basic structure of many letters goes back to antiquity and that they are the direct product of tools and materials that were then available.

The combination of tool and material is clearly demonstrated in one of the earliest scripts, the cuneiform of the Sumerians. Using clay, the most commonly available material, they moulded tablets and impressed wedged-shaped characters into them with sticks. However, cuneiform was a development of an earlier form of writing, the pictograph, which was shared by all the early literary cultures – Sumerian, Egyptian and Chinese – and was a direct pictorial representation of an object. In Egypt, although the imagery came to represent both syllables and more abstract concepts, it retained a strong pictographic content throughout its history. Its use lasted right up to the Roman period and is familiar as hieroglyphics painted or inscribed on tombs and temples.

For everyday transactions the Egyptians produced an equivalent to today's paper by pounding strips of papyrus, readily available on the banks of the Nile, into sheets. Although hieroglyphic writing was used on this, a more fluid script called hieratic, which was written with a reed pen, evolved. This remained the prerogative of the priestly caste and a third script – demotic, the writing of the people – developed for common usage. It too used a reed pen and was quickly drawn.

Phoenicia, also in the Near East, was the site of the next great conceptual breakthrough, in the tenth or eleventh century BC. Of prime importance to all of us, it was the invention of the alphabet, a phonetic system of writing which enables us to reduce speech to a series of symbols, each representing a specific sound. This system spread to cover all the Indo-European languages; Chinese and, later, Japanese writing remained outside this influence. The beauty of the alphabet is that language can be described in some 20-plus symbols as opposed to the hundreds, sometimes thousands, of characters previously used. By the seventh century BC it had been adopted and modified by the Greeks and was in turn adapted by the Etruscans, who gave us our first recognizable alphabet of Latin characters.

The word 'alphabet' is derived from Alpha and Beta, the first two letters of the Greek alphabet. The names of the letters have no meaning in Greek, but in Phoenician the letters of the alphabet were given names. Thus Alpha becomes Aleph, or an ox-head (turn the capital A upside-down and you will get the point), and Beta becomes Beth (Bethel in Hebrew) – a house.

Although most records of these earlier scripts come from inscriptions on stone or pottery, less durable papyrus and wax tablets were in common use. In the second century BC, however, a trade embargo by the Egyptians led the scribes of

Pergamon in Asia Minor to look for an alternative to papyrus. In doing so, they are credited with the invention of parchment. This was to remain the standard writing medium until the technique of making paper reached Europe from China, by way of the Arabs, in the twelfth century.

The introduction of parchment meant it was possible to write and draw in very fine detail, which could not be done on papyrus. The quill pen which could achieve these fine lines now superseded the coarser reed pen. In many ways the use of paper mimics that of parchment, and the evolution of scripts and the use of these mediums can be seen as a continuous development. It could be argued that the principal scripts we use and adapt began to develop during the Roman period when the use of the quill on parchment, and later paper, became widespread. There is, however, one major exception: our capital letters are the product of brush, chisel and stone.

CAPITALS originated as signwritten letters which were subsequently cut into the stone of imperial Rome's monuments. The Imperial capital, the letterform used for these inscriptions was a pure brush-stroke letter. The words were first painted with a broad-edged sable brush and only later carved to make them permanent. The inscriptions on Trajan's column are perhaps the finest examples of the art. The technique used by the ancient signwriters differed very little from that used today. It is important to appreciate this as a basic knowledge of the Roman letter provides the groundwork to understanding most of our capital letters.

Another significant development in the script letter also began during the

Roman period: that of the minuscule, or lower case, letter. This began as a cursive hand that could be quickly written on a wax tablet with a steel stylus. At the same time the early Christians were developing their own script, the Uncial, probably an adaptation of the Greek Uncial. In this, certain characters – the d, f, h, k, l, p, q – had either ascenders or descenders while the a, c and m took on the form of our modern lower case letters. The Roman Empire fell in AD 426 and in the period between this and the evolution of the first true minuscule letter in 780, scripts began to develop independently on a regional basis. The Church was the only unifying factor.

The chaotic state of the West after the fall of Rome was resolved in some measure by the unifying conquests of the Frankish king Charlemagne in the late eighth century. Modelling himself on the Greek and early Roman emperors, he saw the development of learning and culture as the keystones of his empire. In pursuit of his ideal he commissioned Alcuin of York to found a scriptorium at Tours. Alcuin devised a standard writing-hand to be used throughout the empire, based on earlier Uncial and Half-Uncial hands, which in turn had been influenced by earlier cursive scripts. It is known as the Caroline or Carolingian minuscule and this clearly written and easily read letterform – not the later medieval scripts – forms the basis of modern lower case letters.

Over the next 300 years the roundness of the Caroline minuscule became progressively more compressed, and by

CATUS QUEESIONS
ADMOYSENINDE
SERTOSYNAJJNIA
BERNACULOFOE
DERIS·PRIMADIE

From the second Bible of Charles the Bald: the decorated capital is based on a classic Roman letter; the script below it is an uncial. The rest of the script would be in Carolingian minuscule.

about 1100 the original characteristics were all but lost. The next century saw a transition to the Gothic period. In about 1200 the Gothic Textura Quadrata and the Gothic Prescisus scripts, which may be regarded more as inventions than products of evolution, appeared. In many ways they are seen as the embodiment of the Middle Ages and are still widely used especially to suggest anything remotely old, historic or traditional.

To retrace our steps a little, there is one other script that particularly deserves attention and can provide a rich source of both inspiration and material. This is the Insular majuscule. Together with its accompanying display capitals and their amazing decoration, the Insular majuscule evolved from the Half-Uncial, and is probably one of the most beautiful of all scripts. Its development took place away from the influence of continental Europe, in Ireland and northern Britain during the late seventh century. The script itself is not the easiest one to master, but practice can make it one of the most rewarding. With the more easily drawn capitals the interest lies chiefly in their coloured infills and dotted surrounds. The single large capitals or Versals are a treasure-house in themselves – copying even a small section can produce an intriguing and delightful decoration.

The end of the Middle Ages was a period when educated people of intellect looked back to the humanism of Greece and Rome and was marked by a sea-change in the attitude to man's place in the world. By the late fourteenth century, scholars in the cultural centres of Italy were rediscovering the classic works of antiquity. Many of these were, in fact, Carolingian copies but, possibly thinking that they were Roman originals, scribes copied the script in which they were written and, in doing so, evolved a new hand. Clear and unambiguous, it was ideally suited to Renaissance concepts and is now known as the Humanist minuscule. This in turn gave rise to a cursive first cousin: the Italic. A fine example of this script, adapted for modern use and interpreted in a way that suits the current fashion for understated style, is the wall painting on page 54.

The invention of printing with movable type made books widely accessible for the first time – and much of the work of scribes redundant. When it reached Venice in 1467 German printers created new fonts that were more in keeping with local tastes and chose the Humanist minuscule as their model. The typeface they developed was used throughout southern Europe and Britain and is, in principle, the basis of the ones that are most widely used now. Thus we have a direct line of descent from the Caroline minuscule of 780 to the present.

This page of early Italian printing shows a beautiful example of the Humanist minuscule, adapted by the engraver for printed type. The delicate work of the capital E is further proof of the engraver's skill.

A TIMELINE OF LETTERING STYLES AND DEVELOPMENT OF WRITING FORMS

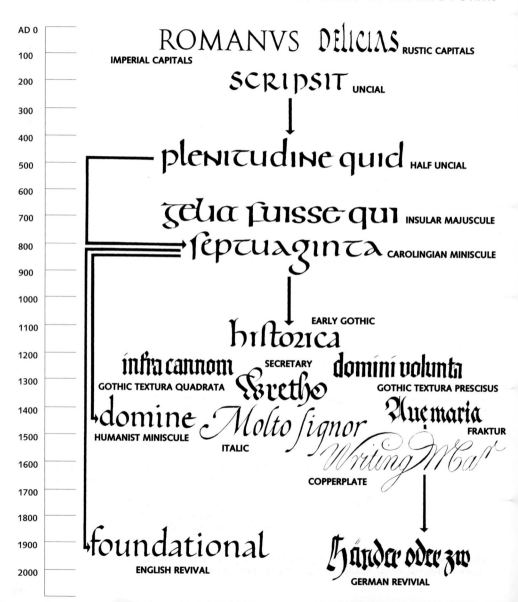

Chisel and brush used for producing signs and monumental inscriptions

Reed brush and pen used for writing on papyrus

Uncial probably devised by ealry Christians for religious writing

Half uncial is a more cursive form of uncial, with ascenders and descenders becoming significant

Fall of Rome and disintegration of Empire
Rise of national and regional hands
Christian church the only unifying factor

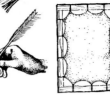

Use of parchment widespread by 3rd century, superceding papyrus. First books, made from folded parchment sewn together, replace scrolls. Manuscripts written with quill

Book of Kells written in *Insular Majuscule*, the writing hand of Ireland and northern Britain

Carolingian Miniscule (AD 780) is the standardised writing hand of the Frankish Empire, based on a reformed half uncial hand by Alcuin of York, centred on the Scriptorium of Tours

Paper-making techniques reach Europe from the Far East via Islam

Invention of printing with movable type by Gutenberg

Decline of the manuscript book

Fraktur deriving from the Gothic scripts, remains in use for type until the 1940s

Secretary is a cursive form of Gothic scripts

Humanist Miniscule, the hand of the Renaissance, is based on the rediscovered Carolingian Miniscule, later used as a model for type by Venetian printers
The *Italic* is a cursive form of the Humanist Miniscule
Copperplate engraving develops by the mid-16th century; *Copperplate* script is a product of the engraver's art

Edward Johnston, pioneer calligrapher, adapted English Carolingian Miniscule as a basic writing hand
German calligraphic revival; Rudolph Koch uses Fraktur script as his model

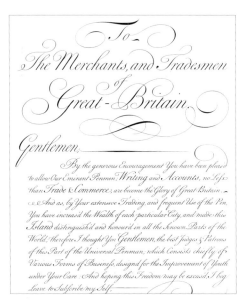

A by-product of printing technology was copperplate engraving which was introduced in the later part of the sixteenth century. The Copperplate script was first developed by engravers as a cursive hand based on the Italic form of the Humanist minuscule. Scribes soon realized that to copy it they simply had to cut their quills to a point. Copperplate had the added advantage that very few pen-lifts were used in its execution, which meant that it could be written at considerable speed while retaining its clarity. By the late seventeenth century it was becoming the

A page from *The Universal Penman* by the renowned calligrapher and engraver, George Bickham. It displays all the elegance of the finest Copperplate. Published in 1743, his book was a manual on the writing of Copperplate.

established business hand and, through the activities of British merchants, was on the way to being accepted worldwide. For many centuries Copperplate script was despised as the hand of clerks and businessmen, and only achieved the recognition it deserves very recently. When William Morris and other designers in the Arts & Crafts movement looked for scripts that reflected their ideals they went back to earlier letterforms.

Modern calligraphy has its origins in the early years of the twentieth century, in the work of pioneers like Edward Johnston in England, who developed the Foundational hand based on the tenth-century Caroline minuscule, and Rudolph Koch in Germany with his Black Letter. They described scripts from antiquity

16

and showed through example the skills involved in constructing them. These had mostly been lost at the time, although in Germany the medieval tradition of the Black Letter continued in type until the 1940s.

To do calligraphy well requires both time and practice, as do all the lettering crafts. But over the last twenty years a series of inventions, starting with the dry transfer and finishing with the word processor, has made near-perfect lettering accessible to everyone. The effect – perhaps in reaction to these mechanized letter-manufacturing techniques – has been to emphasize the skill of designing with letters rather than that of making them. This interest in design and in exploring the forms of handcrafted lettering is the inspiration for this book. It is perhaps a golden rule that the most beautifully drawn letter is wasted in a poor design, whereas an untutored letter can work perfectly in a good one. An example of this is the apparently naïve letterforms, possibly based on roadside

This woodcut initial capital was designed by the German artist Curt Reibetanz in 1925. It has Art Nouveau forms, combined with influences from forward-looking German art movements of the period.

THE BARON SPIDERLEGS COVETS THE BROAD ESTATES OF THE DRAGONFLIES.

A strong influence of the Arts and Crafts pioneer William Morris is seen in this title page, designed by the American Will Bradley in 1896. The origin of the letterforms in the Lombardic capital can be seen most clearly in the letters A, E and G.

A street in London's Notting Hill transformed by graffiti in the style of the artist Jean-Michel Basquiat. Its power lies in the letterforms being drawn with complete freedom, turning the lettering into a striking piece of modern art.

notices of the American Depression, that the late Paul Peter Piech used in his linocut 'Tyger, Tyger'. The result is powerful imagery, befitting its subject.

Modern calligraphers embrace a variety of influences and techniques. These may range from graffiti and using spray paints, to non-Latin hands like oriental, Hebrew and Arabic scripts. There is an increasing appreciation of Arabic calligraphy and the way it has been used in the past, woven into patterns of quite amazing complexity. Perhaps the key to this attitude is the freedom from any kind of doctrinaire approach – and a readiness to explore and search for the aesthetics of any tool, material or tradition that presents itself.

The prohibition on the representation of the human form in Islamic art gave rise to alternative forms of creative expression, producing some of the most beautiful examples of calligraphy and pattern-making.

T R A D I T I O N A L
U S E S

HE STORY OF LETTERING is one of continual evolution. Available materials and practical requirements drive the process of change, which is as apparent in everyday life as it is in the way heroic deeds are recorded and spiritual ideas glorified. Once reading and writing were no longer the province of the educated élite they became a resource exploited by ordinary people in ways that were both creative and practical, and that gave rise to a wonderful variety of domestic art. The ability to read and write conferred status, and even limited skills were valued and used to label possessions and mas-

ter vital documents. Much vigorous and colourful folk art grew out of satisfying simple practical needs and today provides a wealth of ideas and inspiration for lettering artists.

Lettering has often been a focal element in domestic crafts, but nowhere has it been a more integral part of a tradition than in the Scandinavian art of rosemaling, a form of painted decoration. It was applied to many objects, but dower chests provided the prime

This chest, painted by Jocasta for her daughter Tabitha, was inspired by vernacular art forms such as Rosemaling, but she has interpreted the tradition with her own distinctive sense of style.

opportunity for painters to demonstrate their skills. It was important that the chests carried the initials, or full names, of the bride and her father. These became an essential part of the design, which included richly painted motifs of fruit and flowers. Quotations and sayings were used as well as names and dates. The wording would have particular meaning for the family who owned the piece and could be poetry, a religious quotation or a saying that contained a gem of rural wisdom and morality. In Norway, where commemorative inscriptions were the norm on painted furniture, the tradition was to use informal sayings that were specific to

the family. They could be humorous or simply crude, and had to be written in good Norwegian. Rosemaling was used on all manner of household objects, the mundane – an object as humble as a shoehorn could be decorated if it inspired the owner to write a suitable poem – as well as the special. Furniture, plates, tankards and bowls, particularly beer bowls, all received the painter's attention.

A Valdres beer bowl was decorated with the following apt little poem – which unfortunately loses its rhythm in translation. The essence of Rosemaling is this creative marriage of object to witty saying, combined in skilful painting.

A detail of an old Scandinavian dower chest shows a simple painted panel with the typical combination of lettering and plant forms. Handed down through generations, this has the well-worn finish that modern designers strive to imitate.

HEIL OG SAEL; GJER VEL OG SIT.
DRIKK AV MEG, MEN DRIKK MED VIT.

Greetings and happiness; come and sit.
Drink with me, but drink with sense.

The lettering is very much the product of the type of brush used and is recognizable even though there are distinctive variations between artists and regions: each rosemaler developed his own individual style of calligraphy and this was integral to his design. Rosemaling lettering is interesting because it derives not from the Gothic style of neighbouring Germany, but from the English roundhand or Copperplate tradition – in this instance drawn with a pointed brush and not with a pen. The brush is held almost upright to draw the very thin stroke with the tip. It is then angled and its thick part is used to create the bold stems. The letter finishes on the tip. Practice is needed to master this technique but Rosemaling lettering is easier than the more formal Copperplate style. It is full of colourful invention and a source of inspiration for anyone who wants to add vernacular details to an interior.

Scandinavian lettering traditions, along with those of other European countries, reappeared in the New World where they were adapted to new materials and conditions and evolved into lively new art forms. Each group of immigrants made its own contribution to America's developing rural art. An interesting example is Fraktur, a distinctive lettering craft that flourished in the German communities of Pennsylvania for over two centuries from about 1730. The settlers developed a decorative calligraphy inspired by the European art of illuminated manuscript painting, and used lettering that was broadly based on an early Gothic typeface known as Fraktur. People needed documents and Fraktur painting developed in response to this need – each community possessed a teacher or clergyman who was skilled in the art. It began in America's various sects and this is reflected in the religious nature of early subjects: certificates and documents were not painted until later. Book-plates, songbooks, and even Valentines eventually found their way into the repertoire. Many people had a little knowledge of Fraktur because it was taught in the German schools, but the outstanding documents were provided by numerous travelling artists. Early Fraktur reflected its European ancestry in that the inscription was the important element, but as a distinctive American style developed, designs and colours grew bolder and other forms of lettering were occasionally included. Many Fraktur have survived as heirlooms. They provide a wealth of inspiration and are fertile design sources for anyone looking for ideas and motifs that can be adapted to their own style – perhaps to make a family tree that could one day become a treasured possession or, at a less ambitious level, to make greeting cards or a very personal Valentine.

We tend to assume that lettering artists of the past were men but this overlooks the many women who used their needles to record and celebrate their lives. Throughout the history of embroidery, lettering has appeared in a variety of forms. Apart from being decorative, its function was anything from informing and celebrating to recording and labelling. In the context of this book, the shapes of the letters are of particular interest. Most early surviving embroideries were produced for the Church in embroidery schools attached to convents and monasteries and the stitches they used naturally imitated the Gothic lettering of contemporary manuscripts – satin stitch and couched and laid work are perfect for expressing the angular and vertical forms of this script.

Embroidery eventually moved from the convent to the home and the expressions of domestic art that developed as a result are probably the works with most appeal for us. The greatest use of lettering was in samplers, originally the housewife's stitch library. Often named and dated, they contain bands of alphabets whose naïve letterforms are very much in tune with today's taste for historic and vernacular styles. Apart from demonstrating different stitches and the embroiderer's skill, the letters were models for the initials used to label household linens. This simple, practical function developed into the sophistication of the monogram – a mark of refinement as well as ownership. In the project on page 36 we have given a dramatic twist to this tradition by enlarging the initials until they fill the cushion: the monogram has taken on a modern, graphic form.

This birth and baptismal certificate from Pennsylvania, dated 1829, has the beautifully-drawn lettering and decoration of the best Fraktur. Written in German in the New World, it shows the strength of the immigrants' attachment to their traditions.

Whatever the date of an embroidery, the shape of the letters reflects what can be achieved with needle and thread rather than the style of script in common use, and works separated by hundreds of years are united by simple, stitched letterforms. The linear style on the Bayeux tapestry is echoed centuries later in samplers and although the words are in Latin the shapes of the letters are more familiar than those in manuscripts of the time. An English sampler of 1597 uses simple linear outline lettering, and this approach is echoed a century later in an Italian embroidery depicting scenes from Genesis. The background is built up with minute stitches in red silk, and biblical scenes and quotes at the edge are created by lines and patches of bare cloth.

By the mid-seventeenth century, samplers were no longer practical stitch libraries but had become vehicles for displaying sewing skills and female virtues. They could be truly virtuoso pieces of embroidery with many patterns and motifs, alphabets and uplifting quotes. Although their content was increasingly ambitious, the lettering was still restrained by the nature of the stitches – small units like cross- and eyelet stitch were used to build up the shapes, in much the same way that the pixels on a computer screen form the image. This process of creating patterns and texture by repeating a single unit is used for the pincushion on page 46. Letterforms became more decorative and sophisticated in the late eighteenth and early nineteenth centuries as embroiderers used Italic type styles, sometimes with Copperplate-style swashes; a mid-nineteenth century Italian sampler even shows the letters sewn in three colours for an interesting drop-shadow effect.

The graphic invention in embroideries like these should inspire us to look at lettering and layout with fresh eyes. The creator of a sampler in 1797 neatly fitted words into a circle, breaking them to suit the shape. They have been used as an abstract pattern in the same way that words are broken up to fit the doors of the bathroom cupboard on page 74. This is only one example from a number of fine lettering artists whose work is stitched on fabric, carved in wood, painted on walls and china. What they have in common is inventiveness. They have taken traditional forms and used them in their own ways, for their own purposes. And in doing so they have created new styles which, in turn, have inspired new traditions.

T O O L S   A N D
M A T E R I A L S

All the projects in this book need some form of lettering and some require specialist tools and materials, most of which are readily available from art suppliers, good craft shops or local hardware or do-it-yourself stores.

Lettering A number of projects require alphabets. Books on type styles and design are available in the art and design sections of bookshops and libraries – and you can have fun browsing through secondhand bookshops. If you are interested in historic and decorative alphabets there are books in the 'Dover Pictorial Archives' series.

Stationers, office and graphic suppliers and art shops sell transfer or rub-down lettering like Letraset – their catalogues are a good supply of type styles in themselves.

With computers taking over from typesetters, it should not be too difficult to find unwanted type-books and type-sheets.

Both traditional printers and 'quick print' shops have sheets of type specimens; ask them for copies of the ones you want. You will also find that there is a vast range of computer-generated typefaces available on PC's, or from computer bureaus.

Paint and varnish You will need water-based emulsion paint and proprietary colourwash for projects that involve painting or colourwashing walls. To doctor colours, add gouache or raw pigments – a little at a time – or mix with other emulsion paints. Artist's acrylic paints, available in tubes and jars, are also water-based and come in a wide range of strong bright colours and metallic and pearlized finishes. For work on fabric you will require fabric medium, sold in craft shops. This is mixed with paint to give it the right consistency for applying to fabrics, and to enable it to adhere to the fibres and remain flexible when dry. Acrylic varnish is used to seal and protect finished surfaces. It is water-based and is available in matt and gloss finishes. Opaque acrylic enamels and transparent glass paints are specialist products for working on glass.

Keep safety in mind when using paints and solvents. Make sure the room is well ventilated, replace lids on containers and avoid naked flames in the work area.

Inks It is best to use non-waterproof inks for the projects in this book, and for calligraphy in general, rather than waterproof Indian ones as these will quickly clog your pen. The best are Chinese or Japanese. These come in bottles or in the more traditional form of ink sticks, which are ground with water on an ink stone until the required consistency has been achieved. The amount of grounding determines the quality of the finished ink.

Paper You will need a supply of tracing paper for tracing off or transferring designs. Transtrace is a lightweight paper with a chalky surface on one side. Pressure with a pencil transfers a distinct outline, which can easily be removed, to the surface you are decorating. It is easy and cheap to make your own version. Scribble over one side of a sheet of lightweight paper with a 6B pencil to cover it with dense pencil marks; or paint the paper with jeweller's rouge mixed with water. Both papers will last for years. Plain tissue paper is also useful for transferring certain types of design – the pincushion on page 47 is an example. You will need large sheets of strong, lightweight card for making templates and stencil card to make stencils. This is a manila card that has been soaked in linseed oil to make it waterproof. Acetate is a transparent plastic film that can be used on a photocopier. It is also useful for making stencils.

Adhesives Masking tape is essential to hold stencils, etc. in position. Spray adhesive is useful if work has to be held flat and in contact with the work surface. You will need PVA glue for most projects that involve paper. This is a strong, clear, water-based glue that is ideal for découpage and other papercrafts. It can be watered down for using over large areas. Wallpaper paste is a cheap, traditional paper adhesive.

Brushes A range of artist's sable brushes is useful for detailed work. Fine pointed brushes sizes 1 and 4 were used for the muslin curtain on page 64. Lettering like the calligraphy on page 54 and the cushions on pages 36 and 72 require a size 6. Synthetic brushes are cheaper, and adequate for some types of work, but sable ones are more resilient and keep their shape better. They also give extra control for delicate line work.

Larger pointed artist's brushes are useful for painting letters like those on the small lampshade on page 49 or the rosemaling alphabet on page 20. Chinese calligraphy brushes are excellent for these styles as well as traditional Chinese lettering. To achieve the correct letterform both types of brush must be held almost upright to draw thin lines with the tip, then pushed down and angled to paint broad strokes with the thick part. If you want to do brush calligraphy work like Roman Imperial capitals you will need a broad-edged, sable hair or synthetic artist's brush. A brush pen uses ink cartridges and dispenses with pots of ink, making it a very convenient piece of equipment for brush-and-ink work. Stencil brushes have short, thick handles and short, blunt-ended bristles. It is best to work with one that is in proportion to the size of your stencil design. Use a natural sponge for stencilling if you want a more open texture. It will also speed up the process.

For colourwashing and similar work you will need household paint brushes: 4–5 inches (10–12 cm) wide for large areas, 1–2 inches (2.5–5 cm) for smaller ones. A hog's hair softening brush is required for working paint while it is still wet and for moving it around to create soft texture without leaving strong marks.

Pens A range of specialist calligraphy pens – and a number of excellent books on traditional techniques – are available for anyone who would like to try their hand at a little calligraphy, possibly to add the finishing touch to a card and further details of these are given on page 88. However, you don't need specialist equipment to enjoy lettering and to experiment with letterforms. A variety of other tools can be used to make marks: what is important is that you achieve the desired effect. Mapping or draughting pens are useful for fine tracery line work. Felt-tip pens give a free, sketchy look and are readily available in a variety of widths and sizes. You can also use a standard cartridge writing-pen, or pencils – including broad-edged carpenter's pencils – which produce very lively lines.

Cutting tools You will need scissors for cutting both fabric and paper. A good craft knife or scalpel is essential; make sure you have a supply of new blades. Use a cutting mat or piece of thick card to cut on. Always cut against a metal rule or straight edge, or a special safety cutting edge which has a ridge down the middle.

General There are a few pieces of equipment that are useful for drawing, measuring up and setting out a design. Use a ruler to measure your design elements and set them out, and a steel tape measure for larger areas like walls. Marking out large designs like the bedroom wall on pages 55-6 is much easier if you use a plumbline to establish true vertical lines, a spirit level for horizontal lines and a chalk line for marking them on the wall. You will need pencils for drawing up and tracing designs, and tailor's chalk for marking them on fabric. Use transparent red tape to mark positions for a design on glass. A set-square is handy when you are laying out small designs.

A supply of sandpaper and silicon carbide ('wet and dry') paper in a range of grades is necessary for preparing surfaces before painting; and wire wool is used to distress finished effects. Other useful items are: kitchen paper or clean cloths, a palette or old plates for mixing paints, and a staple gun for more permanent fixing.

USEFUL HINTS These general guidelines will help you to plan, draw and execute your designs for the projects in this book.

CREATING LETTER FORMS

The prime consideration in all your work must be to capture the true spirit of the lettering you are representing. Form and rhythm must be mastered and placed within the context of a well-balanced design.

FORMAL SERIF AND SANSERIF LETTERS

If you want to draw correct and precise letters, bear the following in mind:

1 Consistent spacing between letters. They should normally be close but not actually touching. However, you can experiment with different effects like a slightly exaggerated space between letters, a recent typographic trend. Look around and see what the professionals are doing. A good guide is to look at the worst letter combination in a script – an L with an A, for example – and balance the other letter spaces to the space between them.

2 Consistent spacing between words. This is probably less than you think – about equal to the i.

3 Consistent weight of letter strokes. Do remember that rounded letters appear lighter than straight ones, so make rounded strokes slightly bolder; horizontal strokes appear bolder than vertical ones, so make horizontal strokes slightly thinner.

4 Size of rounded letters. These appear slightly smaller than letters with squared terminals or ones with serifs. Correct this by making rounded letters slightly larger.

GOTHIC (QUADRATA) LETTERS

The key to making Gothic letters is to produce an even texture, hence the name Textura. To do this, make sure that the space between each stroke and each letter is as near as possible equal to the width of the upright stroke; the distance between words should be equal to about $1^1/_2$ stroke widths.

MAKING FREE OR INFORMAL LETTERS

The key element here is layout. A helpful suggestion is to trust your eye and sketch in your design freely without using mechanical aids. Pay particular attention to position and margins. It may take a bit of practice before you have the confidence to do this but the results will justify your efforts. Only when you are satisfied with the layout of your design should you consider using mechanical aids in the preparation of your final working sketch.

SCRIPT LETTERS

There are basically two types of script letter: those derived from roundhand or Copperplate scripts; and those drawn freely with a brush. It is advisable to work from a good example of the former; and important to ensure that connecting strokes join the following letter as high up the stem as is practicable rather than near the baseline. The rules for freely-drawn letters are much more flexible – the brush, which can be pointed or chisel-ended, dictates the letterform. Keeping the angles of the letters consistent will help to give the work unity.

TOOLS

1 Work within the range of what your tool can deliver. For example, an old, worn-out brush can produce bold lettering, but don't expect it to create fine detail.

2 A quick, accurate way to produce a series of parallel lines is to hold your ruler or straight edge firmly on the work with one hand and slide your set-square along it while you draw each line.

3 Take great care when you are working with a craft knife or scalpel and follow a few basic rules:

■ Never use a plastic cutting guide; the blade can easily skid on the plastic edge and be deflected towards your hand.

■ Tilt the edge of the knife or the scalpel blade away from your fingers.

■ Use a robust metal ruler or steel straight edge for a cutting guide.

■ Always make sure the blade is sharp and use a series of light cuts. This involves less effort and, because it uses less pressure, will reduce the chances of an accident.

4 Many of the projects in this book specify the size brush that is needed for specific tasks; in others, this will depend on the size of your work.

MATERIALS

1 When working on paper or board always use the best quality available; it is a false economy to do otherwise.

2 Don't use carbon paper to trace down – it will be impossible to erase. Use transtrace transfer paper, or a homemade version (see page 73).

3 Calligraphy nibs write better if sharpened before use. Hold the nib at a consistent angle of 45 degrees and stroke it backwards and forwards over a whetstone (also useful for sharpening scalpel blades).

4 Avoid using waterproof Indian ink for calligraphy. It contains shellac, which will quickly clog your pen.

5 Try making your own pens from items like garden cane, card, felt, lollipop sticks. A whole range of exciting marks can be made with unusual materials.

6 If ink or paint doesn't adhere to the writing surface add a few drops of household detergent.

7 Watercolour, coloured inks and artist's acrylic paints produce translucent effects. Use non-waterproof Indian inks and gouache for maximum opacity.

...e sforze, onde possa dimostrar g...   ...uerente gratiu...

...intti gli effetti Prego pero a V.S...   ...ni fortuna maggic...

...h' ella non haura da desiderar...   ra   ...me osseru più hun...

THE PROJECTS

If you want to explore the creative possibilities of lettering you will find these designs, with their step-by-step instructions, an excellent starting point. There is everything here, from wall treatments to small finishing touches, using materials and techniques as diverse as paper and fabric, gilding and batik.

VICTORIAN VALENTINE

VICTORIAN VALENTINE The Victorians were enthusiastic makers and senders of Valentines and a book of old papercut designs inspired us to create a fresh interpretation of a charming tradition. In our search for an unusual paper we came across this old love letter. The delicate, flowing lines of the faded writing create the perfect pattern and texture for the background, and add an unusual, romantic touch. The heart motif has always been a popular theme in folk art, notably in Scandinavia and Germany. Emigrants from these countries took their crafts with them to the New World where traditional designs reappeared in new and often invigorated forms: the heart motif embellished quilts, stencils and wall paintings throughout Pennsylvania. One attractive example is a Pennsylvania Dutch door of about 1750, with all its panels decorated with hand-painted hearts. The design of this Valentine reflects its simple folk art origins, and relies for effect on the naïve style of the papercut, set against the delicate pattern of the old writing and the soft colour of the tissue paper.

MATERIALS AND EQUIPMENT

pattern for papercut
craft knife or scalpel and cutting mat
lightweight card
old letter or photocopied Copperplate writing or poem
masking tape
pencil
coloured tissue paper
PVA glue
old corks
artist's acrylic paint: gold

Note If you don't have an old love letter, photocopy an example of Copperplate writing. Or find a suitable poem – make sure, though, that it is set in a typeface that produces a pleasingly decorative pattern when used as a background.

We made an envelope from another copy of the love letter and decorated it with a little gold stamping. Make it even more special by sealing it with gold sealing wax.

2 Make 2 photocopies of your letter or photocopied writing and cut them into identical squares. Carefully fold one of them in half, and then half again. Put the template in position on top of the folded letter, hold it in place with masking tape and draw around the shapes with a pencil. Remove the template and cut around the pattern, through all 4 layers of paper. Repeat this process with the second photocopy.

1 Photocopy a pattern with a simple shape that divides naturally into quarters or can be joined up to make a 4-cornered repeat like this one. It should not be too complicated as all the little shapes will have to be cleanly cut out. Adjust the pattern on the photocopier until you are happy with the effect. Use a craft knife or scalpel to cut a template of the pattern in lightweight card.

4 Draw hearts and your initials and those of your loved one on old corks, then use a craft knife or scalpel to cut around the shapes so that just the raised images are left. Now dip these stamps into gold paint and stamp the Valentine with these motifs.

3

4

3 You will see your design appear as you unfold the papercuts. Paste the coloured tissue to the back of one of the 2 papercuts with PVA glue. This is when the pattern really comes to life. Trim the tissue to the edge of the paper and paste the second papercut to the other side of the tissue, matching up the corners.

MONOGRAMMED CUSHIONS

We have taken the idea of mono-grammed linen and given it an exciting new twist. There is nothing understated about these cushions. We chose a 'swash' italic typeface for the monogram and enlarged it to fill the whole cushion – we wanted to make the most of the graphic qualities of the letters. We made the pattern on one of the cushions even more elaborate by extending the letters into decorative swashes and filling up the spaces around the monogram with gold tracery.

MATERIALS
water-based fabric
   medium
artist's acrylic paint: gold
fabric for cushion covers
sheet of paper
stencil card

EQUIPMENT
typeface for monograms
tracing paper and pencil
spray adhesive
masking tape
craft knife or scalpel
   and cutting mat
tailor's chalk
artist's sable brush, size 6
iron
equipment for mixing
   fabric medium and
   paint

The burnt orange and cinnamon of these fabrics combine richly with the gold lettering on the cushions, to add a celebratory look to this autumnal interior.

36

1 Choose a typeface, bearing in mind that a curving style will work best for this design. Trace off the letters for your monograms and group them together on a sheet of paper to form a decorative pattern. Secure the letters in position with spray adhesive or tabs of masking tape, then lay a fresh sheet of tracing paper over them and trace them off. Enlarge your design on a photocopier until it fits the cushion then trace it onto stencil card. Outline the design in pencil and use a craft knife or scalpel to cut a stencil of the monogram.

2 Cut the fabric to fit your cushions, then lay it flat on your work surface and secure it with masking tape. Place the stencil on top of the fabric and hold it in position with masking tape and a little spray adhesive. Draw the monogram design around the inside of the stencil with tailor's chalk.

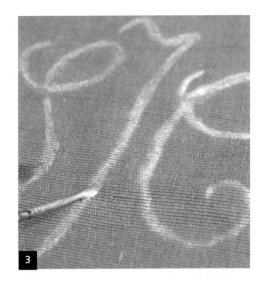

3 Mix the fabric medium with the gold paintaccording to the manufacturer's instructions. Remove the stencil and, following the design marked out in tailor's chalk, paint the lettering with the artist's brush.When the paint is dry iron the back of the fabric using a medium setting. This will fix the pattern and make it permanent and washable. Make up the cushion.

4 Repeat this method for a second cushion, but have a bit more fun this time. Once you have drawn the letters in tailor's chalk and removed the stencil, extend the ends of the letters to fill the spaces on the cushion with decorative doodles.

DÉCOUPAGE BATHROOM FRIEZE Designer Linda Barker shows how effective simple techniques can be. She has used découpage letters to create an unusual frieze which provides a subtle focus to this bathroom. The design takes advantage of the abundance of typefaces that computers now make available to us. We have adapted this as an ideal project for anyone who is unsure of their painting skills: the lettering requires nothing more than computer-generated type and a pair of scissors. Choose bold, simple shapes that are easy to cut out and that create an even pattern when they are pasted together. An upright Roman face is more suitable than an Italic script; select one with a strong, clear outline. It is important to get the letter and word spacing right. Remember to keep it to a minimum (see the guidelines on page 28) and practise laying out the lettering before you start pasting.

see the guidelines on page 28

MATERIALS
computer-generated typeface (see above)
white or cream paper
paint(s) for colour-washing
chalk line
wallpaper paste

EQUIPMENT
decorator's sponge
hog's hair softening brush
spirit level
scissors

Note The colour of your lettering must harmonise with your wall. We used a dusty pink colourwash mixed from Paint Magic Buff, Mango and Fresco Pink.

The gentle colours and worn surfaces of this room give it an air of cool tranquillity. The colourwashing blends the frieze into the dusty pink tones of the wall and softens the outline of the letters to a muted grey. Because the words are in Latin the frieze is seen as pattern and design rather than lettering – which makes it all the more intriguing.

TUTE VIDERIS ESSE QUI NOSCAT REM BONA

1 Decide on the 3 important elements in your design: the typeface, the size of the lettering and its position on the wall. Print out the lettering in the correct size on white or cream paper, depending on the base colour of your wall.

2 Sponge the colourwash onto the letters with a decorator's sponge, then use a hog's hair brush to soften the pattern on the sponging – try to create an effect that is similar to the finish on the wall.

3 Mark the distance of the line of type from the floor and use a chalk line and spirit level to check that it is horizontal. Now mark the base line for your letters with the chalk line.

4 Cut up the letters with scissors and glue them into position with wallpaper paste.

KITCHEN LABELS Making labels for kitchen jars is a good way to learn about type styles and will give you practice in drawing them. Antique labels will provide inspiration or you could find interesting lettering in old type-books. Start with the simpler letterforms and avoid the more elaborate script faces which can look much more decorative but could be difficult to master. See page 28 for guidelines on working with different type styles as well as how to space letters and words.

MATERIALS
typeface(s) for labelling
tracing paper and pencil
white paper
tissues or crumpled
  newspaper
glass paints or acrylic
  enamels

EQUIPMENT
black felt-tip pen
kitchen jar
artist's sable brush, size 2
Blu-Tack or reel of
  masking tape

Building up a collection of storage jars can be fun. Look out for interesting ones in junk shops and don't throw away used jars without checking to see whether they have any potential.

Try to get as much variety as possible into the design of the labels. Copy old ones or design your own using the blanks overleaf.

1 Choose the type style for your label and enlarge or reduce the letters on a photocopier to fit your design. Trace the words onto white paper and then darken the lines of the lettering with a black felt-tip pen. This gives you a strong line to follow when you paint the lettering on the jar.

2 If you want borders around your labels (which can be either painted directly onto the glass or traced onto paper and pasted to the glass), you may want to use the designs we used in the picture on page 42: see designs opposite for templates.

3 Trim down the paper and position it inside a jar against its side. Push tissues or crumpled newspaper behind the trace to hold it in place.

4 Following the trace, use an artist's brush and glass paints or acrylic enamels to paint the lettering on the jar. Keep the jar steady with lumps of Blu-Tack or by resting it at an angle in the middle of a reel of masking tape as a cradle.

LABEL TEMPLATES

VICTORIAN PINCUSHION Inspired by captivating examples in a country museum, this charming keepsake shows how the natural desire to embellish and be creative can find expression in even the smallest details of people's lives. While intended for decorative, not practical use (keep out of children's reach), the messages worked on Victorian pincushions indicate that they were gifts for special occasions like a birth or a christening. The pins used in the originals have faceted heads which add a slight sparkle to the texture they create. The trimming was often lace, but silk fringing, fine cord, ribbons and little tassels could be used, and as you will need only the smallest of scraps of fabric for the cover itself. This would be a neat way to use up little remnants of old silk from a treasured dress.

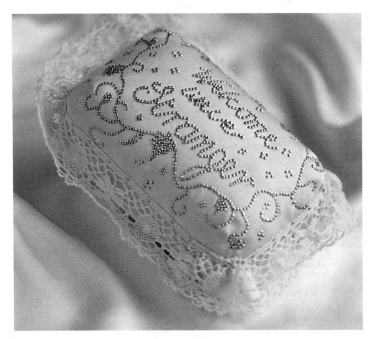

MATERIALS
calico
sand or bran
tissue paper
a scrap of pale silk or
    satin
old lace, for the edging

EQUIPMENT
needle and thread
pins (2 boxes
    approximately)
scissors

Much of these pincushions' appeal is in their simplicity: only the base shape is stitched; everything else is done with pins. For the best effect, use lots of them to form a dense pattern against the delicate fabric.

1 Sew a miniature cushion shape in calico and leave one end open. Turn it inside out, fill it with sand, then sew up the end. Push in the corners to round and soften the shape, then hold in place by oversewing them with a couple of stitches.

2 Work out a design that will fit the cushion and transfer it onto tissue paper.

3 Position the silk or satin over the top of the little cushion and pin it in place around the edge. Lay the tissue paper with the design on it over the cushion and hold it in place with pins. Now start building up the design with the pins, pressing firmly down into the cushion.

Once you have established the basis of the design you can remove the tissue paper by tearing it away from the pins. Continue building up the design until you are happy with the way it looks. For the best effect, be generous with the pins.

4 Cover the bottom of the cushion with a piece of plain silk or satin. Again, hold it in position with pins around the edge. Trim off the surplus fabric with scissors.

5 Finish off the cushion by trimming the edge with a delicate ribbon of old lace. Ease the lace around the corners of the cushion by making little gathers in it and hold it in position with more pins.

'CHINESE' LAMPSHADE This lampshade is proof that inspiration is all around us if we keep our eyes open. The starting-point for this project was nothing more exotic than the menu card from a Chinese restaurant. The characters, which mean 'Golden Jade', have strong shapes and work well as stencils. The drop shadows give extra emphasis and a three-dimensional effect to them; we stencilled the lettering in two colours, one over the other, and shifted the top one slightly to the right. It isn't difficult to find examples of Chinese characters – they may even be on bottles and packaging in your local supermarket. I returned from Chinatown, after the mid-autumn festival, the proud owner of a fine piece of Chinese calligraphy: my name written in Chinese characters. I am still wondering where to use it.

MATERIALS	EQUIPMENT
Chinese characters	craft knife or scalpel and
tracing paper and pencil	cutting mat
stencil card	masking tape
plain card lampshade	stencil brush(es)
artist's acrylic paints:	1 inch (2.5 cm) varnish
black, red	brush
matt or gloss acrylic	
varnish	

Note If you only intend to stencil your characters a few times, use the photocopy paper instead of stencil card. It will last long enough if you give it a couple of coats of matt or gloss acrylic varnish for protection, and it will bend easily around the lampshade.

The lamp-bases were chosen to go with the styles of two very different lampshades. The chunky, 'oriental' earthenware base complements the boldness of the Chinese characters, while the graceful glass column on the left is in keeping with the traditional elegance of the groups of script and letters on the shade.

1 Choose your Chinese characters. (It might be a good idea to know what they mean!) Trace the characters with tracing paper, then enlarge them on a photocopier and trace them onto stencil card. Cut out stencils with a craft knife or scalpel.

2

1

2 Secure the stencil around the lampshade with tabs of masking tape, then stencil the characters in black first with a fairly dry stencil brush.

3 When the black paint is dry, use a clean brush to stencil the same characters with the red paint. Shift the stencil slightly to the right of the black characters to create the drop shadows. When the paint is completely dry, brush on a protective coat of acrylic varnish.

LETTERED LAMPSHADE This elegant lampshade makes clever use of the patterns and textures created by contrasting letterforms. The most important element in achieving success is to have an overall sense of the design; this far out-weighs the skill with which the letters are drawn. Set large letters against areas of small script, and use a variety of different type styles while maintaining an overall harmony – keep an eye on the balance of the design.

Note If you are uncertain of your drawing skills you can achieve a similar effect with a quick découpage version. This is simplicity itself. Photocopy the selected samples of script and cut out the sections to be used. Work out the design by positioning the pieces of lettering around the shade, then hold them in place with tabs of masking tape and mark their positions. Paste the pieces of script in place using diluted PVA glue, and leave to dry. Stain the shade lightly with tea to give it a pleasantly aged look, then seal it with a coat of matt or gloss acrylic varnish when it has dried.

MATERIALS	EQUIPMENT
selection of type samples	transtrace transfer paper
tracing paper and pencil	masking tape
plain parchment	Chinese brushes: 1
lampshade	medium and 1 fine
artist's black ink	1 inch (2.5 cm)
matt or gloss acrylic	varnish brush
varnish	

We used Chinese brushes and black waterproof ink to paint the lettering, but you could use a large artist's brush or a brush-pen and artist's black acrylic paint. Use the medium that suits the style of lettering you have chosen.

3 Use Chinese brushes and black ink to paint in the lettering following the trace lines. When the ink is completely dry, brush off any transtrace chalk with a clean soft brush. Seal with a protective coat of acrylic varnish.

2

3

1 Gather together an interesting collection of type samples and select the ones you want to use. Make sure you have a good variation of patterns and sizes. Trace your chosen samples onto separate pieces of tracing paper.

2 Work out where you want the different blocks of lettering to appear on the lampshade and mark off the areas in pencil. Put a piece of transtrace paper over one area and position the relevant tracing over it. Hold in position with tabs of masking tape. Draw over the shapes of the letters to transfer them to the shade. Continue doing this until all the lettering has been transferred.

...mi consolo d'hauer hauuto

be... debole una tal robu

per superar le mie forze, onde possa dimostrar g... riuerente gratitudine

con le conditioni tutti gli effetti Prego pero a ... fortuna maggiore
asseurandolo, ch'ella non haura da desiderar m... me o necu più humile...

WRITING ON THE WALL Lettering adds a poetic touch to this romantic bedroom. The walls were colourwashed to mimic the colour and texture of old faded plaster, and the diamond shapes (see over) were sponged in a paler wash over this background colour to make a sympathetic background for the soft grey lettering. The Renaissance feel of the room is enhanced by the choice of the early Italian script known as the Humanist minuscule. The Italic form used here is the cursive development of the hand which later evolved into Copperplate. The designer has successfully captured the pattern of the words with rhythmic changes of emphasis in the brush strokes. The lettering has a natural flow and pattern: broken lines and irregularities are all part of the aged look that gives this room its very special atmosphere. It does not matter that the words are written in Latin: in fact, it helps us to see the lettering as pattern and texture, and to appreciate its fine graphic qualities. See over for our interpretation.

The plasterwork plaque on the wall and the old four-poster bed with its faded, distressed paintwork have been chosen to complement the antique style of this interior. It is a good idea to experiment and try out your painting technique on a small panel. Remember that imperfections do not matter. It is more important to capture the essential qualities of a letterform and to do this with an eye to the overall effect of the design.

MATERIALS

chalk line
lightweight card for
    template
paint(s) for colourwashing
    and diamonds
lettering
artist's acrylic paint for
    lettering
matt acrylic varnish to
    seal

EQUIPMENT

spirit level
plumbline
chalk
masking tape
decorator's sponge
hog's hair softening brush
acetate
overhead projector
    (see page 57)
artist's sable brush, size 6
3 inch (10 cm) decorator's
    brush for varnish

template top to bottom and draw around it to create the bottom half of the diamond. Now turn the template the right way up, sit it on the horizontal line next to the first diamond and match its widest point with that of the diamond. Draw the diamond shape as before. Repeat along the wall to complete a frieze of diamonds.

3 Mask off the diamond shapes with masking tape. Mix a paler wash of your background wall colour and sponge it onto the wall with a decorator's sponge. Work quickly and freely across the diamond shapes, then use the hog's hair brush to work the wash while still wet.

1

2

3

1 Measure your wall and decide on the size of the diamond shapes and how many you will need. Divide up the length of the wall to fit the number of diamonds. Decide where to position their centres, then measure up from the skirting to this level. Use a chalk line and spirit level to mark this horizontal line. Establish the vertical centre line of the first diamond with a chalked plumbline.

2 Use lightweight card to make a triangular template that is the size of half a diamond. Sit the template on the horizontal line and align it with the chalked vertical line that marks the centre of the first diamond. Draw around the template with the chalk. Turn the

The colour of your diamonds will depend on the background colour of your walls. We used a paler wash of the mixture used for the walls – Paint Magic Antique White, Buff and Fresco Colourwash – for the diamonds, and artist's pale grey acrylic paint for the lettering.

FACILIS DESCENSUS AVERNO:
NOCTES ATQUE DIES PARTET ATRI JANUA DITIS.
SED REVOCARE GRADUM, SUPERASQUE EVADERE
   AD AURAS,
HOC OPUS, HICLABOREST.

Easy is the descent to Avernus;
Night and day stands open the gate of gloomy Pluto;
But to recall the step, and pass out to the upper air,
This is the toil, this the labour.

VIRGIL

4

5

4 Continue working with the hog's hair brush. This will soften the pattern of the sponging and move the paint around to create a worn, mellow texture.

5 Photocopy your chosen text onto acetate and use an overhead projector to project it onto the wall; adjust until the size and position look right. Water down the artist's acrylic paint to get a flowing consistency, then start painting the lettering with the artist's brush. Work quickly to achieve a good rhythm: it is this rhythm and pattern in the writing that is important – don't worry about imperfections, they're all part of the charm. An overhead projector can be hired, or borrowed from an art college or friendly photographer.

COUNTRY-STYLE TABLE MATS This project is much easier than it seems at first glance and is worth trying if you want to make table mats that fit in with a particular colour scheme or set of china. We chose a simple, black-and-white print-room theme that would look at home in a country-style kitchen or dining room. You may wish to experiment with other patterns and themes – but bear in mind that this technique is best suited to naïve 'woodcut' images.

MATERIALS AND EQUIPMENT
old table mats
calico (pre-washed to shrink, and ironed smooth)
acetate
photocopying paper
brush for applying image transfer medium
image transfer medium
cloth pad
scouring pad
PVA glue

You could use this technique to make mats for a whole range of special occasions – a child's party, for example, when you might want something that is quick to make and can be thrown away later. In this case, don't mount the calico on base mats; just fringe its edges or trim them with pinking shears.

2 3 4

over and make a photocopy on paper. The image will be reversed.

2 Brush the reversed image on the paper liberally with the transfer medium.

3 Place the coated paper face down on a piece of calico and rub across it with a cloth pad. Press down firmly when you do this. Leave to dry for about 4 hours, overnight if possible.

4 Wet the paper with water and use a scouring pad to scrub it away from the calico. The image will remain in place. Give the calico prints a light wash and cover your table mats with them when they are dry. Glue them in position with PVA glue, wrapping the fabric over the edge of each mat. Snip the calico at the corners to ease it around the shape.

1 Use an old table mat as a template and cut the calico into the required number of pieces. Remember to add an allowance for wrapping the fabric over the edge of the mats. Choose your images and photocopy them – enlarge them if necessary – onto the acetate. Now turn the acetate

BATIK CUSHIONS: HOMAGE TO THE EAST

If you feel inhibited when you work with traditional lettering tools, making these striking cushions will allow you to have fun. Drips and unplanned dribbles of wax add to the pattern and the spontaneous look of the finished cloth, so concentrate on keeping the wax flowing and on getting a good rhythm in the lettering. We used a 'tjanting', a traditional batik tool (see page 63). It consists of a handle with small bowl, the reservoir for the melted wax, on the end. A long, thin spout emerges from the base of the bowl. The type of wax you use will affect how it flows from the tjanting and the look of the finished cloth. Special batik wax is available from craft shops or you can mix your own. A good general purpose one consists of 1 part beeswax to 3 parts paraffin wax. A higher proportion of paraffin wax in the mix makes it more brittle and its melting point higher. It will also be more difficult to keep a good flow of wax going. The more brittle wax is used to produce special crackle textures.

These colourful cushions look strikingly modern although the fabric has been produced using an ancient technique. The lettering has become a wonderfully abstract pattern of line and texture, full of free movement which adds another dimension of meaning to the words. Experiment with different colours and other batik techniques.

MATERIALS	EQUIPMENT
calico	frame
quotation	masking tape, double
batik wax or a mix of	sided tape or staples
1 part beeswax to	pencil
3 parts paraffin wax	double boiler
brown paper	tjanting
newspapers	cold-water dye and
	container
	iron

2 Melt the wax in a double boiler. Dip the tjanting into the hot wax to fill the reservoir. If the wax cools down too much while you are working its flow will slow down or become erratic. If this happens, just dip the tjanting back in the hot wax.

3 Dribble the wax onto the calico with the tjanting. Follow the lines of your lettering and don't worry about drips and irregular, wobbly lines. They add to the texture and pattern of the finished fabric.

4 Following the manufacturer's instructions, make up enough cold-water dye to soak the fabric. Remove the fabric from the frame and drop it into the dye. Leave it for about an hour – or longer, depending on the dye you are using.

1 Stretch the calico over a frame and hold it in position with masking tape, double-sided tape or staples. Choose your quotation and decide where to position the words, then lightly pencil them onto the fabric.

5 Place brown paper on both sides of the fabric and put on a pad of newspapers. Now iron the paper and fabric sandwich on a high setting. The wax will melt out of the fabric onto the brown paper. You will need quite a few changes of paper before all the wax has gone. (It might be best to use an old iron for this step.)

Note If you don't have a frame for stretching the calico use a box, an old tray or even the top edge of a drawer.

6 Hand-wash the fabric in warm water, then dry and iron it. Make up your cushion.

COME EVERY STEEL BLADE,
AND EVERY STRONG HAND
THAT BEARS ONE.

'The Gathering Song of Donald the Black', Sir Walter Scott

2 3
5
4

REGENCY-STYLE MUSLIN CURTAIN

As designers rediscover the beauty of lettering in all its forms, classic type styles as well as hand-written scripts are making their appearance on walls, furniture and fabrics. They provide ideas and inspiration for anyone who wants to use lettering as a design feature in their home. This curtain, inspired by a reproduction of an old document from the Royal Pavilion in Brighton, echoes the beautiful white-and-gold theme of the north drawing room.

The title page of the document is an interesting example of the engraver's art and demonstrates in a few lines some of the influences that have played their part in the evolution of scripts. Copperplate engravers of the period often used a variety of type styles and adapted them for their own purposes, sometimes with little regard for the correct structure and use of the letters. The main title of the document is written in a form of Fraktur, a style of Gothic script, which has been

MATERIALS	EQUIPMENT
white muslin	tailor's chalk
old lettering	masking tape
gold acrylic paint	acetate
water-based fabric medium	equipment for mixing paint and fabric medium
	artist's sable brushes, sizes 1 and 4
	iron
	fabric protection or fire-retardant spray (optional)

White muslin, evocative of the graceful neo-classical dresses of the Regency period, is a fashionable fabric for this type of work. Our muslin curtain looks best with the light shining through it to reveal the lettering. Used like this, in front of a window, it is a stylish way of creating a little privacy. This idea can be used more lavishly, perhaps as drapes around a bed.

elaborated with traditional Copperplate 'swashes'. The decorated capital letters are also based on Fraktur but, as with the small ones, the engraver's art has come into play. The left side of each letter has been highlighted and a line and dot decoration incorporated, creating the effect of a shadow on the right side. Engravers of the day had no inhibitions about mixing typefaces, and this title page is no exception. Here the modified Fraktur is combined with the classic Copperplate Italic script of the second and third lines. The word 'King' on the last line is an engraver's adaptation of a Tuscan letter, italicized and with added swashes. A Tuscan letter is basically one which has slab serifs and splits half-way down the stem with double or triple curved serif feet. Usually drawn in outline, with a shaped or coloured infill plus internal and external shadows, these letters are tremendous fun to make. They were great favourites with fairground proprietors for the whole of this century and much of the last.

Old documents like this one often contain interesting examples of Copperplate script with all its exquisite curves and swashes. If you are hunting for sources of old lettering look for old deeds, household books and accounts, and manuscripts, certificates, wedding invitations and diaries.

1 Make up a muslin curtain to fit your window. Work out the best size and position for the lettering and lightly mark the layout on the curtain with tailor's chalk. Enlarge your lettering on a photocopier until it is the required size. Keep a spare photocopy for testing the consistency of the fabric medium and paint mixture (see Step 3).

2 Stick the photocopy to your work-table with masking tape and cover it with acetate to prevent the paint sticking to the photocopy. Secure the muslin in position over the acetate with small tabs of masking tape.

3 Mix the gold paint with the fabric medium. It should have a good flowing consistency without being too runny. Paint a few test pieces on some scraps of muslin. When the paint and your brush-work are flowing smoothly, start painting the lettering directly onto the muslin. Use the size 1 brush for fine lines and the size 4 for broader ones. Wait for the paint to dry, then lift the muslin and move it to the next position. Paint on the second set of lettering. Repeat the process until the muslin is covered. When the paint is dry, iron the back of the lettering using a medium setting. This will fix the pattern and make it washable. You may need to use a fabric protection or fire retardant spray on your curtain.

DECORATIVE FOOTSTOOL This pretty little footstool was a trophy from a successful rummage in a junk shop. It seemed a good location for an amusing quote and, with a little time and effort, it turned into a very special gift. The typeface we chose has attractive, curving, 'swash' capital letters, in keeping with the shape and style of the footstool. We found some decorative corner motifs in a type-book to complete the panel design. The technique of using a 'dropped' shadow gives a three-dimensional effect to the lettering. It is important to remember that this kind of shadow should be treated as if it were cast by the lettering and should always appear on the same sides of all the letters. Practise on a scrap of fabric to perfect your letter shapes before you tackle the design proper.

HE SITS
NOT SURE
THAT SITS
TOO HIGH

A Dictionary of Quotes

The rich-coloured cushion with its gold lettering gave a tired piece of furniture a new lease of life and the gilding on the frame completed the opulent look. We used Dutch metal transfer leaf for this as it is cheaper and easier to use than true gold leaf – and can be just as effective.

MATERIALS	EQUIPMENT
quotation	craft knife or scalpel and
tracing paper and pencil	cutting mat
spray adhesive (optional)	masking tape
fabric for cushion pad	artist's sable brush, size 2
board or strong card	equipment for mixing
artist's acrylic paints:	paints and fabric
gold; dark colour for	medium
'shadows'	iron
fabric medium	fabric protection or fire-
	retardant spray
	(optional)
	staple gun

2 Draw the shape of the cushion pad on tracing paper. Cut up the words with a craft knife or scalpel and position them in the shape of the panel on the cushion pad. It is important that they create a balanced design. Look carefully at the spaces between the words. It is all too easy to allow too much space between them, so move them around until the design looks right. Decide where to position the corner flourishes. Secure the words and flourishes in position with spray adhesive or masking tape.

1 Measure the footstool cushion pad and decide on the area to be filled by the quote. Select a suitable typeface for your quotation, then trace off the letters and enlarge them on a photocopier. Keep spare photocopies to test the consistency of the paint and fabric medium mixtures.

69

3 Lay a fresh sheet of tracing paper over the words and trace them off. Make sure you include the corner flourishes.

4 Cut the fabric to fit the cushion pad. Allow enough over to wrap it around the pad and attach at the back. Stretch the fabric over a piece of board or strong card and hold it in position with some masking tape.

5 Turn the tracing paper over and draw over the letters in pencil on the reverse side. Place the tracing of the quotation right-side-up on the right side of the fabric. Scribble over the lettering and corner details with a pencil to transfer the lines from the reverse side of the trace onto the fabric. Press hard when you do this.

6 Now apply the decoration. It is best to start with the darkest colour in the design, so mix the dark acrylic paint with the fabric medium until it has a flowing consistency without being too runny. Paint a few test pieces on some scraps of fabric to check. Then use the artist's brush to paint the drop shadows on the left sides of the letters and the corner details.

7 Now that you have laid the foundation of the design with the shadows you can move on to the more exciting part of the job. Mix the gold paint with fabric medium as in Step 6, then complete the panel by painting in the letters and corner motifs. Leave to dry then iron the back of the lettering using a medium setting. This will fix the pattern. You may also want to use a fabric protection or fire-retardant spray.

8 Stretch the fabric over the cushion pad and staple it to the board on the back with the staple gun. Replace on the footstool.

5 6
7

NORWEGIAN CUSHION The inspiration for this cushion was a trademark in an old book of Norwegian wallpapers. I was attracted by the strong shapes of the lettering and could see its potential as the basis of a bold design. Look around for commercial graphics that have the same simple unity: an old tin lid, for example, or signs, cards, matchboxes, advertisements or clothing labels. Continental and Asian food stores are a favourite hunting ground of mine for original packaging and labels, and old newspapers are another rich source of ideas – I have found some unusual typography in advertisements of the 1900s.

The colours of this cushion harmonize with the other natural colours in this setting. You could repeat the technique in different fabrics, colours and trimmings and then group the cushions together for dramatic effect. We used plain raw silk, but try heavy cotton or calico, with a cord edging or piping.

MATERIALS

lettering (see above)
tracing paper and pencil
fabric for cushion cover
artist's acrylic paint: red
water-based fabric
    medium
fringing, cord or piping
    (optional)

EQUIPMENT

spray adhesive
masking tape
equipment for mixing
    paint and fabric
    medium
artist's sable brush, size 6
iron

1 Measure your cushion and decide on the size of your lettering. Enlarge the original lettering on a photocopier. You may have to do this in sections and piece them together to achieve your required size. Keep a spare photocopy to test the consistency of the paint and fabric medium mixture.

2 Stick the photocopy to a window with a little spray adhesive and masking tape for an easy way of lighting the pattern clearly from behind. Place a sheet of tracing paper over the top of this and trace the outlines of the letters so that you have a strong clear outline to work to.

3 Position the fabric over the tracing and secure it with tabs of masking tape. Mix the paint with the fabric medium until it is flowing well without being too runny. Paint a few test pieces on a spare photocopy and some scraps of fabric. Now brush over the traced lettering with the artist's brush and fill it in. Allow the paint to dry, then iron the back of the fabric using a medium setting. This will fix the pattern and make it permanent and washable. Finally, make up the cushion cover. Add a fringe, cord or piping, if you wish, to complete the effect.

TE LA
MP VA
US RE

CUPBOARDS: CLASSIC AND VERNACULAR

Lettering on furniture has a long vernacular tradition. It has been used for practical purposes like labelling the contents of a cupboard or drawer or identifying the owner of a piece, and for commemorating important family events as well as for decoration. Here it has transformed standard cupboard doors into something special as well as helpful. The simple technique of découpage lettering has produced two very different looks. The choice of typeface is the key: the Roman capitals on the bathroom cupboard have a classic elegance well suited to this treatment, while the rounded upper and lower cases of the 'Pots & Pans' have a more traditional appeal. The use of outlines and drop shadows emphasizes the letters and creates a three-dimensional look. The method is the same for both cupboards.

MATERIALS
masking tape
lettering in your chosen typeface
sheet of white paper
wallpaper paste
matt acrylic varnish

EQUIPMENT
ruler and pencil
craft knife or scalpel and cutting mat
artist's sable brush, size 6
2 inch (5 cm) varnish brush

Opposite: The lettering makes full use of the graphic forms of Roman capitals. Linda Barker's design disregards the normal arrangement of the words TEMPUS LAVARE ('time to wash') and concentrates on how the letters are positioned within the space. Because the phrase is fragmented we no longer focus on its meaning – instead we become aware of the pattern of the letters.

Above: The upper and lower case typeface is friendly and readable, ideally suited to the cupboard's farmhouse kitchen setting. Drop shadows give an interesting relief effect to the letters.

1 Measure your cupboard doors and work out where you want the lettering to go and what size it should be. Mark the positions for the words with a ruler and pencil.

2 Enlarge the lettering on a photocopier. Place a sheet of white paper under the photocopied lettering and hold it in position with tabs of masking tape. Use a craft knife or scalpel to cut through both sheets of paper. This will produce identical letters in black and white.

3 5
4

3 Use an artist's brush to paste the black letters in position on the doors with wallpaper paste.

4 Now paste the white letters in position over the black ones. Shift them slightly to the right to create a three-dimensional shadow effect.

5 When the letters are completely dry, seal the door with a coat of matt acrylic varnish.

SILVER GILDED MIRROR

SILVER GILDED MIRROR This beautiful mirror frame by artist Alexandra de Zoete is inspirational – an ambitious but highly rewarding project. True water-gilding is time-consuming and requires skill and practice, but the result is very special and well worth the effort. The simple sculptural quality of the lettering that builds up the border around the frame is the result of brushing on layers of gesso. Silvering can be shiny, even brash, when it is first applied. The mellow effect here was achieved by distressing the finished surface with wire wool and then tarnishing the silver with egg white. Silver leaf invariably tarnishes as a result of oxidation, so this trick makes a virtue of necessity.

MATERIALS
wooden mirror frame
sandpaper
dusting brush
gesso (see page 87)
saucepan of hot water
silicon carbide paper,
    medium- and fine-
    grade
lettering
yellow clay (see page 87)
blue clay (see page 87)
silver-gilt leaf
petroleum jelly (optional)
gilding water (see page
    87)
cotton balls
agate burnisher
white of hard-boiled egg
beeswax

EQUIPMENT
tracing paper and pencil
masking tape
artist's sable brush, size 7
clean cloths
hog's hair brush(es)
gilder's pad, knife and tip
fine steel wool
white polish
methylated spirits

never seek to
tell thy love,
love that never
told can be

WILLIAM BLAKE

This mirror is a work of art that would add a touch of opulence to any setting. It looks particularly fine here in Jocasta's home where the deep-glazed walls provide the perfect background. If you are gilding for the first time, it would be best to test your skills on a smaller panel initially.

NEVER SEEK TO
TELL THY LOVE,
LOVE THAT NEVER
TOLD CAN BE.

1 Prepare the frame and rub it down with sandpaper. Clean all traces of dust from the frame with the dusting brush: it is important to keep it free of dust at all stages of the work. Make up some of the gesso: stand it in a saucepan of hot water to keep warm and apply 8 coats to the frame with the hog's hair brush, brushing on evenly and allowing each coat to dry before applying the next. Leave the frame to dry, then rub down the surface of the gesso, first with medium-grade silicon carbide paper and finally with fine grade. Dust the surface with the dusting brush.

Work out the design for the lettering, and trace the letters that will make up the quote. Secure the tracing paper to the frame with tabs of masking tape and transfer the design. Paint the shapes of the letters with the gesso. Use an artist's brush and build them up one layer at a time. Allow the gesso to dry between coats. When you have built up enough relief, smooth the tops of the letters with a slightly damp cloth and finish very lightly with a dry one to buff up the relief. Use the dusting brush to remove all the dust from the surface.

2 Heat up the yellow clay and keep it warm over a saucepan of hot water. Use a clean hog's hair brush to apply 2 coats of the clay to the frame so that it covers the gesso completely. Allow the clay to dry between each coat. Heat up the blue clay and apply 2 coats as above. Allow to dry. Rub down the surface with fine-grade

silicon carbide paper until it is smooth. Clean the surface with the dusting brush.

3 Now gild the frame, working on small sections at a time and tilting it at a slight angle to allow the gilding water to run down the frame. Drop a leaf of silver-gilt onto the gilder's pad and use the gilder's knife to cut it up into pieces that will fit the areas you are working on. Pick up a piece of leaf with the gilder's tip (a very small amount of petroleum jelly on the end makes this much easier). Hold the loaded tip in one hand and paint the area to be gilded with the gilding water – work fast because the gilding water will dry in a few seconds. Now apply the leaf to the sized surface, and pat each leaf down onto the surface with a ball of cotton wool to get rid of air bubbles. Continue until the whole mirror is gilded. Burnish the raised letters with an agate burnisher.

4 To distress the silver-gilt, rub the surface with fine wire wool, working with a circular movement until the clay starts to show through, but do not rub away too much away. Break up the egg white into small pieces and drop in a random pattern onto the silver gilt to tarnish it. Leave for about 5 minutes, or until you have the degree of tarnish required, then brush off lightly, removing the last traces with a clean cloth to prevent further tarnishing. Seal the gilded frame with an even coat of white polish, wax lightly with clear beeswax and buff with a clean cloth.

SIGNWRITING: A TRADITIONAL

ART Modern innovations like peel-off lettering and computer graphics threaten to put an end to a skill that has been practised since Roman times. Signwriting is not easy but we included this project because we wanted to stimulate interest in an important traditional craft – and also because hand-painted signs offer creative opportunities and visual variety in an increasingly uniform environment that is dominated, more and more, by mechanically generated letters. Signwriting on glass calls for skill and experience, so practise and experiment before you begin work in earnest; it is best to start with a small project – possibly your house name and number on the fanlight over your front door.

MATERIALS
sheets of paper
tracing paper
lettering
paints (see page 84)
gloss acrylic varnish
    (optional)
mahlstick (see page 84)

EQUIPMENT
masking tape
transparent red tape
brush(es) for applying
    paint (see page 84)

Above: this striking and very individual sign, the final result of our signwriter's work, gives a dramatic finish to one of the doors at Paint Magic's head office. The lettering appears to be floating, unattached to the glass panel – an intriguing illusion.

1 Work out your design and indicate the positioning of the lettering on a sheet of paper. Trace your chosen letters and enlarge them on a photocopier until they fit your design. You may need to do this in sections and piece the sheets together. Trace the design onto a sheet of paper, then secure it to the outside of the glass with masking tape so that you are looking at it in reverse as you work. Use lines of transparent red tape to mark the top and bottom of the letters. Although this is not essential, it will ensure a precise edge when the tape is removed and allow you a degree of overpainting.

writing opaque. Allow the paint to dry between coats. Note how the signwriter uses the mahlstick to steady and support his painting hand as he works.

3 Apply the final protective undercoat followed by the varnish; you don't need to follow the outlines of the letters precisely with the varnish coat but can slightly overlap them.

2 Apply the first coat of paint – the colour required for the finished design – with an artist's brush. When the glass is lit from the back the brushmarks will become visible, so you will need to overpaint a number of times to make the

Note Make sure your drawing is accurate; you will be working in reverse and it can be difficult to tell whether letter shapes are good when you are looking at them back to front. Paints are applied in reverse order on glass: what would normally be the final coat is put on first and the undercoat last.

SPECIALIST EQUIPMENT FOR SIGNWRITING

PAINTS: OPAQUE LETTERING

Household paints and craft products like acrylic enamels are all suitable. Consistency is vital: the paint must be fluid enough to flow easily without clogging the brush but it must not be so thin that it runs off the glass. It must also be opaque enough to allow you to paint a solid letter with the minimum number of coats. Use an oil-based paint for exterior work that will be exposed to the elements. Oil-based undercoat is the most opaque of all paints and you can modify its consistency with white spirit and gold size. Add a few drops of linseed oil to restore fluidity if it dries out too quickly. Household emulsion paints can be used for interior work but they are not as opaque as the undercoat and may gather into globules; remedy this by adding a few drops of detergent. There is also a range of paints designed specifically for signwriting.

Intermix paints to achieve the colour you want, or add artist's oil colour thinned with linseed oil to oil-based products and gouache to emulsion ones.

PAINTS: CLEAR LETTERING

Transparent glass paints, available from craft shops, allow light to shine through lettering, as in stained glass work.

PALETTE

An artist's small palette is ideal. Its detachable cups hold the small amount of paint that is usually required.

BRUSHES

Good brushes, preferably in a range of sizes, are essential. Traditionally made of red sable, they should produce a fine square edge when wet. A signwriter's 'pencil' has longer and more flexible bristles than most chisel-ended brushes sold in craft shops. It is more difficult to use but will prove rewarding with practice.

MAHLSTICK

This specialist equipment is a stick about 12 inches (30 cm) long with a soft, padded end and is available from good craft shops. Alternatively, you can make your own with a length of dowel and padding – which should ideally be covered with chamois leather. The mahlstick's main function is to provide a steady support for the hand and allow a greater range of movement. It can also be used as a straight edge when drawing vertical and horizontal lines. Signwriters usually hold the palette or paint pot in their mahlstick hand.

IDEAS FOR THE FUTURE

As the projects in this book have shown, art can evolve out of the simplest materials – in the 1930s the artist Ben Nicholson based a design for a scarf on a humble bus ticket – and you may well be excited enough by the possibilities of lettering to be inspired to use it in ways that are completely your own.

If you want to make lettering an element in interior design you will need plenty of time to plan your scheme. Start by throughly researching your script and make sure you can make a satisfactory copy of it. If you want to create the atmosphere of a particular period the lettering style must be of the correct date even if you use it in a modern way. Experiment with techniques. You can even distress the finished effect so that it looks as if the wall is crumbling away.

Fabric offers great possibilities in an interior. A whole range of techniques, from the free lettering used for the batik cushions on page 62 to crisper shapes that can be made with stencils or stamps, is at your disposal. The softness and movement of fabric lends itself to flowing, informal shapes and their fragmentation, produced by the fabric's folds, would further enhance an abstract treatment. Always work within the possibilities of a material. You will get a far better result if you exploit its natural properties rather than work against them.

Paper is the natural material for experiments with lettering – it comes in wonderful colours and surfaces and is relatively inexpensive. Start by playing with freely painted letters and cut or stencilled shapes. Try different mediums on paper. Choose a rich-coloured paper or card and paint a message in a water-based gilding size (or PVA glue for a less permanent effect). When this is nearly dry, but still tacky, lay a piece of gold or silver leaf over it and press down so that the leaf adheres to the varnish. Now brush off the loose metal leaf to reveal gold or silver lettering against the coloured background. Paste cut-out letters on a flat surface to create changes of colour and texture or build the shapes up in layers to make three-dimensional letterforms.

Take rubbings of lettering – remember to ask permission first – and add them to your library of interesting typefaces or use them to create your own wrapping-paper or cards. If you are lucky enough to find a source of old documents or letters you can experiment with decoupage effects. Exploit the pattern and texture of the writing by using photocopies of the manuscripts as an aged background for old photographs.

The possibilities are endless. Whether you are attracted to the traditional uses of calligraphy or want to follow more recent trends in design, you will be making your own creative contribution to the art of lettering.

GILDING RECIPES

RABBIT-SKIN SIZE

2 oz (50 g) rabbit-skin size granules

1 pint (600 ml) water

Pyrex bowl

saucepan of water

Mix the rabbit-skin size granules with the water in a bowl. Put the bowl over a saucepan of water, then bring the water slowly to the boil and simmer gently. Stir the rabbit-skin size mixture until all the granules have dissolved. Leave to cool. To use, reheat the size over a saucepan of hot water until it melts.

GESSO

Buy whiting in powder form and mix with the rabbit-skin size (above) and water.

2 parts rabbit-skin size (see above)

1 part water

pyrex bowl

saucepan of water

whiting powder

Mix the softened rabbit-skin size with the water in a large metal bowl. Put the bowl over a saucepan of hot but not boiling water. With the saucepan off the heat, sieve the whiting powder into the rabbit-skin solution until a little island of powder appears at the surface. Stir until the mixture is smooth, then sieve through a fine sieve or pair of nylon tights. Keep the gesso warm while it is being applied.

YELLOW CLAY

1 part rabbit-skin size (see above)

1 part water

Pyrex bowl

saucepan of water

yellow clay (from artist's suppliers)

Mix the softened rabbit-skin size with the water in a bowl. Put the bowl over a saucepan of hot water. When the solution is warm, add enough yellow clay to achieve a creamy consistency.

BLUE CLAY

1 part rabbit-skin size (see above)

2 parts water

Pyrex bowl

saucepan of water

blue clay (from artist's suppliers)

Follow the instructions for making up yellow clay.

GILDING WATER

Gilding water dries very fast, in a matter of seconds. It is therefore vital to gild small areas at a time and to work fast.

methylated spirits

$^1/_2$ mug water

rabbit-skin size (see above)

Add just enough methylated spirits to the water to colour it. Melt a little rabbit-skin size and add a drop to the solution in the mug.

C A L L I G R A P H Y

To learn more about traditional calligraphy techniques you should consult one of the many specialist books available. The traditional tools are, of course, quills and reed pens, used since the earliest days of writing, although on page 27 we have suggested some modern alternatives. But quills and reed pens can be very rewarding to experiment with, and some of the lettering styles on the following pages would be suitable for freehand copying using these traditional implements (although you could equally use the lettering templates to spell out a saying, motto or series of initials of your choice and blow it up on a photocopier to trace or use in découpage).

CALLIGRAPHY TOOLS

The reed pen produces the most expressive work, while the quill is one of the finest tools. However, a lot of practice is needed to master it. There are several types of steel pen-nibs. The most widely used and commonly available is known as the dip pen. It is broad-edged and is suitable for most calligraphic work. The ink is held between the matching front and back halves of the nib. The square-cut nib, known as the 'slanted' pen, is cut at right angles to the shaft and is held at an angle of about 30 degrees. The most commonly used of the specialist pens, it is suitable for most scripts and ideal for ones like the Gothic Quadratas. The oblique-cut nib, confusingly known as the 'straight' pen, is the most specialized calligraphy pen and the least used. The nib is cut at an angle of 70 degrees to the shaft and is held in a horizontal position. It is most suitable for scripts like Insular majuscule. Finally, there is the pointed Copperplate nib which is used for drawing Copperplate script.

SAMPLES
OF LETTERING
STYLES

'LOMBARDIC' CAPITAL

ABCDEFGH
IKLMNOPQ
RSTUXYZ ✳

ROUND HAND (COPPERPLATE)

abbcddefoghhiijkkllmnnoppqrsfstuvwxyz.
ABCDEFGHIJKLMMM
NNOP2RSTUVWXXYZ.

DAINTY

ABCDEFGHFI

IJKLMNOP2RS

TUVWXY3

FARGO

ABCDEFGHI

JKLMNOPQR

STUVWXYZ

&.,;:- 9 6699 ¡?

NORWEGIAN SCRIPT

A B C D E F G H I J K L
M N O P R S T U V W Y
a b c d e f g h i j k l m n o p r s t u v x y 1972
A C D E O Olav Tore N I

FRAKTUR

A B C D E F G H I J
K L M N O P Q R S T U
V W X Y Z a b c d f g h i j k l
m n o p q r s t u v w x y z

ABCDEFGHIKLM

NOPQRSTUVW

XYZ

abcfghijklmnopqrs

tuvwxyz

ABCDEFG
HIJKLMN
OPQRSTUV
WXYZetc.&

Resources and Further Reading

The Alphabet and Elements of Lettering F.W. Goudy, Dover Publications, Inc. 1942

American Folk Decoration Jean Lipman, Dover Publications, Inc. 1972

The Art of Calligraphy David Harris, Dorling Kindersley 1995

Calligraphy Donald M. Anderson, Dover Publications, Inc 1969

Calligraphy Georg Schwander, Dover Publications, Inc. 1958

Calligraphy: Art & Colour Peter Halliday, B.T. Batsford Ltd 1994

Calligraphy – Inspiration, Innovation and Communication David Harris, Anaya Publishers Ltd 1991

Lettering and Alphabets J. Albert Cavanagh, Dover

Letterwork Brody Neuenschwander, Phaidon 1993

Norwegian Rosemaling: Decorative Painting on Wood Margaret M. Miller and Sigmund Aarseth, Charles Scribner's Sons 1974

Ornamental Alphabets & Initials Alison Harding, Thames & Hudson 1983

The Royal Pavilion Brighton The Royal Pavilion, Art Gallery and Museums, Brighton

Signwritten Art A.J. Lewery, David & Charles 1989

Treasury of Calligraphy edited by Jan Ischichold, Dover Publications, Inc. 1984

The Universal Penman engraved by George Bickham 1743, Dover Publications, Inc. 1954

The Dover Book Shop
18 Earlham Street
London, WC2H 9LN
tel 0171 836 2111
stocks an extensive list of books on type, calligraphy, and historic and modern alphabets, and has a full mail order service.

PAINT MAGIC SHOPS

Paint Magic offers a complete range of decorative paints, traditional ingredients, brushes, stencils and books. Each branch also offers weekly courses in decorative paint techniques.

PAINT MAGIC
MAIL ORDER
79 Shepperton Road
Islington, London
N1 3DF
United Kingdom
tel (0171) 226 4420
fax (0171) 226 7760

PAINT MAGIC
ARUNDEL
26 The High Street
Arundel, West Sussex
BN18 9AB
tel (01903) 883653
fax (01903) 884367

PAINT MAGIC
BELFAST
59 The High Street
Holywood,
County Down
BT18 9AQ
tel (01232) 421881
fax (01232) 421823

PAINT MAGIC
GUILDFORD
3 Chapel Street
Guildford, Surrey
GU1 3UH
tel (01483) 306072

PAINT MAGIC
ISLINGTON
34 Cross Street
Islington, London
N1 2BG
tel (0171) 359 4441
fax (0171) 359 1833

PAINT MAGIC
NOTTING HILL
5 Elgin Crescent
Notting Hill Gate,
London W11 2JA
tel (0171) 792 8012
fax (0171) 727 0207

PAINT MAGIC
RICHMOND
116 Sheen Road
Richmond, Surrey
TW9 1UR
tel (0181) 940 9799
fax (0181) 332 7503

UNITED STATES

Paint Magic products are stocked by Pottery Barn branches across the United States. For details of your nearest stockist, call Pottery Barn customer service (800) 922 9934, or write to:

POTTERY BARN
MAIL ORDER
DEPARTMENT
P.O. Box 7044
San Francisco, CA
94120-7044
tel (415) 983 9887

CANADA

PAINT MAGIC
CALGARY
101, 1019 # 17th
Avenue SW
Calgary, Alberta
T2T 0A7
tel (403) 245 6866
fax (403) 244 2471

ISRAEL

PAINT MAGIC
TEL AVIV
255 Dijengoff Street
Tel Aviv 63117
tel (972) 3605 2476
fax (972) 3544 5710

SINGAPORE

PAINT MAGIC
SINGAPORE
Seik Yee Paint Shop
30 Watten Rise
Singapore 1128
tel (65) 463 1982
fax (65) 463 1982

FURTHER DETAILS

There are more Paint Magic shops opening worldwide in the near future. Please call or write for our catalogue, price list, Design and Decoration Service and details of the latest shop to open near you.

PAINT MAGIC
HEAD OFFICE
77 Shepperton Road
Islington, London
N1 3DF
United Kingdom
tel (44) (0)171 354 9696
fax (44) (0)171 226 7760

First United States Edition

First published in Great Britain by Macmillan, an imprint of Macmillan Publishers Limited

ISBN 0-8212-2453-0

Library of Congress Catalog Card Number 97-71567

Bulfinch Press is an imprint and trademark of Little, Brown and Company (Inc.) Published simultaneously in Canada by Little, Brown & Company (Canada) Limited.

Series Origination: Jocasta Innes
Text and Research: Jane Forster

Design: Hammond Hammond

Original Photography:
Marie-Louise Avery, Sue Baker

Artwork pages 14-15 by David Harris
Stencil lettering page 93 by Andrew Meade

ACKNOWLEDGEMENTS
Grateful thanks to David Harris, whose knowledge and love of the written word has provided a continual source of information and inspiration. His contribution, particularly to the historical section, was invaluable.
Thanks are also due to the signwriter Tony Veers for his contribution to the signwriting project on pages 82-3, and to Alistair Little for permission to photograph the lettering in his restaurant, featured on page 1.

Joacasta Innes also wishes to thank:
Project Manager: Sarah Curran
Assistants: Sammy Dent, Tim Tari,
Sacha Cohen, Thandi McPherson
Senior Commissioning Editor for
Boxtree/Macmillan: Gordon Scott Wise
Editor: Tessa Clark

PICTURE CREDITS
Marie-Louise Avery 1 (except inside right), 2-3, 19, 25, 31, 33, 34-5, 36-7, 40-1, 43, 44, 46-7, 60, 62-3, 66-7, 68-9, 70-1, 76-7, 78, 80, 82-3, 84-5; Sue Baker 1 (inside right), 30, 39, 42, 49, 50-1, 52-3, 54, 56-7, 58-9, 65, 72-3, 74-5, 79; Sammy Dent 18; Paint Magic 20, 95

Printed in Italy